NO EYE HAS SEEN

NO EYE HAS SEEN

NO EYE HAS SEEN

Christ for all Nations *Great Gospel Crusade* Season 2002/2003

No Eye Has Seen © Rob & Vanessa Birkbeck, 2003 ISBN 0-9536488-3-4

Published by International Images, rbirkbeck@intlprojects.org
On behalf of Christ for all Nations (CfaN)
P.O. Box 590588, Orlando, FL 32859-0588, USA. www.cfan.org

All photographs, other than those acknowledged on page 87 © CfaN/Rob Birkbeck
Other photographs © Christ for all Nations, used by permission.
Text compilation: Rob Birkbeck. Design and layout: Vanessa Birkbeck & Lisa Parkes
Final origination and printing: China Printing Corporation, Beijing, China. Set in: Futura T & Papyrus

Scripture quotations are taken from the Holy Bible, New International Version (NIV), Copyright © 1973, 1978,
1984, International Bible Society and used by permission of Zondervan Bible Publishers, Grand Rapids, USA

Other books by Rob Birkbeck:
A Picture of a Moment in Time ISBN 0-9536488-1-8
Carried in your Heart ISBN 0-9536488-2-6

Printed in China

Authors' Introduction

During the 2002/2003 *Great Gospel Crusade* season, the Christ for all Nations team witnessed over 7,000,000 people ushered into the Kingdom through the work of the ministry.

Many of our valued prayer partners around the world see the images of huge crowds of up to and including 1,600,000 people in a single gathering, which have become synonymous with Evangelist Reinhard Bonnke. Yet, few have had the opportunity to see what goes into the making of such an event, the cities that they impact, and the dedicated team that works to put it all together. Our desire in producing this book is to take the reader 'behind the scenes' to see things from a different perspective. *No Eye Has Seen* is a collection of images taken by a number of CfaN photojournalists, who have been privileged to be on the spot to capture history in the making, and yet have taken the time to meet some of the people whose lives have been changed as a result of a CfaN crusade.

The title of the book comes from 1 Corinthians 2:9, 'No eye has seen, no ear has heard, no mind has conceived what God has prepared for those who love Him.' Between the two of us, we have visited over 110 countries, and seen the world's most wonderful sights; yet, looking down on the sea of faces and hearing countless souls cry to God with one voice, is surely the most amazing sight and awesome sound we have ever witnessed.

During these last sixteen years, as part of the ministry, we have seen and experienced the Father's love, grace, provision, and mercy in ways that we truly could not have conceived. He is truly good to His word, yesterday, today, and always.

Rob & Vanessa

Rob & Vanessa Birkbeck

Dedication

We dedicate this book to Reinhard and Anni Bonnke and all fellow members of the worldwide Christ for all Nations team. People from different backgrounds, nationalities, and races, yet all bound together in fulfilling a single vision—to preach the gospel message across the length and breadth of the continent of Africa, and to reach the world with the good news of Jesus Christ. No words can express the extent of our love and respect for you all.

What momentous times! Ever since God gave me the vision of a blood-washed Africa, 'Africa shall be saved!' has burned in my heart. We, at Christ for all Nations, are experiencing such a harvest of souls like never before. It seems to me that we are witnessing how God is answering the prayers of generations of Christians, and how He honors every seed sown with abundant reaping.

I have so often longed to be able to take every prayer partner on a crusade. Now, through the wonderful pictures in this book, you are about to take the journey with us. So much has been captured of the commitment and excitement of our crusades. There is no greater joy than to experience the roars of praise that ascend from a crusade crowd who have just witnessed God's mighty miracle-power at work. All the people whom you will meet in the following pages will show you this joy.

Jesus said, 'Go...!' This we do with all our hearts because people come, listen, and experience that Jesus saves, delivers, and heals – this is our driving force.

Thank you for praying for us.

Reinhard Bonnke

From the planning stage, which begins about a year before the event, to bringing in the harvest, every CfaN crusade is the sum of many parts. After years of gospel crusades, the CfaN staff has become experienced in both the organizational and spiritual demands of such an event.

(Top Right) Kwame Biney and Lucy, both of the CfaN West Africa staff.

(Left) Vanessa, Kwame, and Blessing preparing one of the massive promotional billboards for an upcoming event.

(Right) God has given Christ for all Nations great favor, and open doors are rich opportunities for soul-winning.

The face of Africa is a hungry one—not only for what the market place provides, but also for the 'Bread of Life' Himself.

The local market is the heart of any city. It is where people come to meet, and where, nowadays, the news of CfaN's coming travels faster than the local media! So much so that a walk downtown often leads to calls of 'Are you Bonnke?'

'And they noised it far and wide that He was in the city'. In the weeks prior to the crusade, local taxis, burdened with the weight of loudspeakers, crisscross the city announcing the crusade. On every house, shop, and bus stop, posters and CfaN calendars are the decor of choice.

'Blessed is he who comes in the name of the Lord!'
The arrival becomes a convoy of jubilation as the evangelist arrives in the city.

After the drive from Lagos, Reinhard Bonnke is first welcomed by the entire crusade committee and senior local church leaders then, at the entrance of the city, by tens of thousands of enthusiastic welcomers.

A triumphant drive through the city follows, usually accompanied by bands playing, scores of motorcyclists, and dozens of speaker-toting taxis all announcing the *Great Gospel Crusade*. The city streets are lined with promotional teams waving banners and distributing flyers, plus hundreds of people and smiling school children.

In the weeks leading up to the crusade, the event has been advertised on television, on the radio, on tens of thousands of posters, dozens of huge billboards, and hundreds of thousands of handbills.

An entire city is made aware of the *Great Gospel Crusade.* Promotional teams work with all types of media to cover the event. Every newspaper that wants to increase its readership and every radio station that wants to be heard will cover each day of the crusade in detail.

In many African cities, Reinhard Bonnke is welcomed as an honored guest at the Royal Palace.

(Above) The King of Ile-Ife, Oba Okunade Olubuse II and his wife.
(Above right) At an evening pastors' and leaders' meeting before the crusade, Evangelist Bonnke is presented with a royal garment by the Queen of Ondo Town.
(Center right) His Royal Majesty, The King of Ado Ekiti.
(Bottom right) His Royal Majesty, Oba Festus Ibidabo Adesanoye. Owemowe of Ondo Kingdom, and his wife.

Weeks before every crusade, the first part of the technical team arrives, and begins to prepare the ground. Working with local authorities, they select an open area accessible and suitable for such a gathering. Often a virgin site is chosen, one that has perhaps been earmarked for a new market, building site, or agricultural use, but, because of lack of funding, it remains overgrown. CfaN covers the cost of clearing the site, and building access roads. When the crusade is over, it is handed back to the local community for their use.

By the time the international team arrives, most of the preliminary technical work is complete. The ground has been cleared, and the sound systems are in the final stage of construction. Reinhard Bonnke comes down to the site to visit, and to gather the team together for a time of prayer.

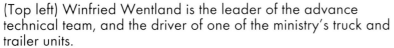

(Top left) Winfried Wentland is the leader of the advance technical team, and the driver of one of the ministry's truck and trailer units.

(Top right) Martin Jocham starts up one of the site generators.

(Bottom right) Derek Murray, CfaN's technical director, checks speakers before they are hoisted into position.

(Opposite page) David Hopkinson installing one of the many light towers around the platform and campaign ground.

From the construction of the mobile platform for the optimum position on the crusade site to the setting up of the numerous musical instruments and countless microphones, every aspect of the technical side has to be double-checked and made to work before the first night.

(Top) Derek assembling and checking equipment at the foot of each sound tower.

(Center) Alan Gibson setting up the worship group's microphones and equipment feeds, while (Bottom) Nathan Kemp assembles musical equipment.

(Opposite) The old sound system looking upwards. After 14 years of constant use in harsh conditions, it has now been upgraded.

With 24 new laser-guided speaker boxes, together with eight
speakers from the old sound system, the new combination
can push out in excess of 90 decibels of raw sound. It
includes 8,800 pounds of equipment, and miles of cables,
all of which are hoisted into the air by 16 electric motors
on the two 43-feet-high aluminum towers spaced 50 yards
apart. Each loudspeaker is linked by a computer network
to the control room enabling its performance to be remotely
monitored and adjusted.

People gather from every part of the city. Some have traveled for days, on foot, by bus, or by overloaded taxi. They come by any manner of transport, anxious to hear the preaching of the word of God, and expecting to witness for themselves the signs-following gospel. Close to the time of the crusade, local roads are blocked off to normal traffic as all access routes are packed with celebrating and singing crowds. It is like seeing an entire city on the move.

(Above) At dusk, the evangelist arrives down a dusty road especially cut through the bush as a back access for the team. The people have gathered in the cool of the day, and now they are ready to hear a fiery gospel message.

(Left) The King of Ondo Town is welcomed to the platform by Reinhard Bonnke. He is delighted to see him in the royal garments presented to him when he arrived in the city.

(Top right) The King of Ile-Ife, Oba Okunade Olubuse II and his wife during one of the meetings.

(Right) Siegfried Tomazsewski, Evangeline van den Berg, Peter van den Berg, and Evangelist Reinhard Bonnke.

In order to count such a huge crowd of people, the entire campaign ground is first divided up into a number of sections, usually demarkated on the field by the light poles. Then, while the crowd is quiet during the preaching of the word, one person is sent out to measure the density of people per square metre/yard within each section. The totals of all sections are then added together to give a grand total. It is impossible however, to count and include all of the people in overspill areas, adjacent roads etc as well as the many in vantage points like trees and on rooftops!

Great Gospel Crusade in Ogbomosho, Nigeria. November 6-10, 2002.
1,758,144 souls saved (Decision cards completed ready for follow-up).

(The white lines are strings of ushers and security put in place to contain and manage the huge crowd)

(Above) Part of the Ogbomosho Crusade massed choir.
Often in excess of 1,000 members, the choir from all
participating churches joins voices with one heart.

(Right) The sound control desk is nested within the huge
crowd, like a boat on an ocean of humanity. From there,
all sound levels are constantly monitored and adjusted
by Nathan, the field sound engineer.

(Previous page)
Owo Great Gospel Crusade.
Part of the crowd of two hundred thousand
people that surged into the campaign ground
each evening. Despite political elections and
fuel shortages, the people still came to hear
the message of salvation using every means of
transport, some simply walking for many miles
down dusty roads.

Alongside every *Great Gospel Crusade* the
ministry hosts a *Fire Conference,* which attracts
delegates from across the local region, some
traveling for days to attend. Reinhard Bonnke's
heart is to challenge all those present to engage
in 'Evangelism by Fire', God-given Holy Spirit
Evangelism. He proclaims that 'an unpreached
gospel is no gospel at all'.

(Right) The Ogbomosho *Fire Conference*. 'Forty
thousand heads and a flame for every head!'

Evangelist Bonnke shares his heart on the things that continue to fire his vision as delegates take in every word. *'The proper purpose of Pentecost is to get the wheels rolling for God in every church, thereby transporting the gospel across the face of the whole earth.'* The *Fire Conferences* have become an integral part of all *Great Gospel Crusades* and have inspired many new evangelistic ministries. *'During the day the delegates are taught, and during the night they see for themselves the potential that God has placed in each and every heart! The gospel is eternal, but we don't have eternity to preach it ... we have only as long as we live to reach those who live as long as we live!'*

The largest stadium in Ondo Town is the venue for the packed *Fire Conference*. Forty thousand delegates from all denominations and church groups open their hearts to the Holy Spirit at the Saturday morning meeting, the climax of the three-day pastors' and leaders' conference.

Thirty-five thousand delegates from across the region
crowd into the Makurdi sports facility. They are eager to
hear what drives Evangelist Bonnke to Holy Spirit
evangelism, so that they too may be inspired to reach
their nation with the signs-following gospel.

(Right) CtaN's West Africa Director, Rev. John Darku, encourages the *Fire Conference* delegates to open their hearts, and prepare for the speakers of the day, Rev. Reinhard Bonnke and the ministry's Vice Chairman, Rev. Peter van den Berg.

(Far right) Peter van den Berg delivers a powerful message on *The Crisis of Faith*.

(Below) Sound Engineer, Greg Szabo fine-tuning the conference sound system to ensure that all 40,000 delegates can hear clearly.

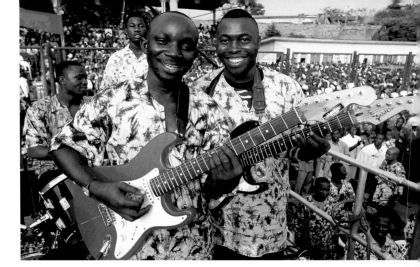

Local musicians and singers 'in one accord', joyously lead the delegates in praise and worship.

(Above & right).
The Anointing Service, the climax to the Ile-Ife *Fire Conference.* A mighty united roar is heard across the gathered crowd as every delegate prays in new tongues.

'The fire is not to save us trouble in winning the world; it is to empower us to preach the gospel in spite of trouble. Revival fire is not a reward for good people. It is God's gift.'

Full-time and freelance CfaN photojournalists and television crews capture the highlights of every event in order to communicate to prayer partners around the world the report of how God is moving across the nations. (Above) Adelmo Raymann (Right) Kai-Uwe Bonnke (Far right) Bent Würslin (Below) Rob Birkbeck

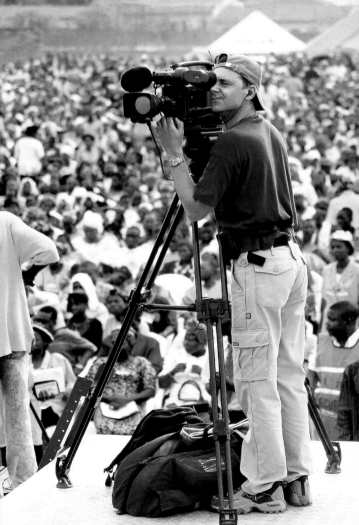

On the final day of every *Fire Conference*, each delegate is given a personal copy of Reinhard Bonnke's book *Evangelism by Fire*. Hundreds of thousands of books are given away every year at such gatherings. This ensures that, long after the event is over, the written word will remain to encourage, uplift, and inspire. Millions of copies of the same book are distributed free of charge during literature 'seeding' projects in various other parts of the world.

(Left) Delegates at the Makurdi *Fire Conference* wave their copies of

Over 1,042,024 people received Jesus as their personal Savior, completed a decision card during the Ondo Town *Great Gospel Crusade,* and were connected to one of the 110 local participating churches.

The technical team forms an important and vital connection between the preacher and the people. From the back of the huge campaign ground, some 650 yards from the platform, the message can still be heard clearly. An area the size of 96 soccer fields can be reached with the ministry's new sound system, used for the first time in Ado Ekiti.

(Right) Because of traveling vast distances, the team is self-dependent, and the containers provide an ideal on-the-road kitchen and dining space. Gerhard and Lawrence enjoy a break during the day's busy schedule.

An integral part of every *Great Gospel Crusade* is the follow-up work done by the army of counselors (some times as many as 200,000 at a single event!). Armed with copies of the campaign literature *Now that You are Saved* translated into the local languages, the details of all new converts are recorded, and passed onto the local church. During the 2002/2003 crusade season alone, some 7,370,222 decisions were recorded in this way. To date, an amazing total of over 63,000,000 copies of this booklet have been printed in over 50 languages.

High above the gathered crowds, the sound system and lighting towers frame Vanessa in the 'Genie', which is an observation platform that rises straight up from the otherwise featureless crusade around giving an excellent vantage point.

Sudden agitation by small groups in the crowd, followed by thunderous shouting and praising, identify healings within the huge gathering. As the gospel is preached, signs and wonders follow. The lame walk, the blind see, and people are healed from all kinds of disabilities and sicknesses.

(Above) This woman is challenged to touch Bonnke's ear as a demonstration of being healed of blindness. (Right) This man's speech has been restored after being totally dumb for 8 years.

(Left) Jesus came to set the captives free! This young man came with a number of witnesses onto the platform to testify how God had healed him from insanity. The huge gathering roared its approval as Bonnke cut the chains that held him.

The technical support systems required for the organization of each *Great Gospel Crusade* are immense. Sometimes, as many as ten containers are hauled across the country and grouped together to form a virtual 'village'. These containers are then transformed into storerooms and specially equipped support modules, which house all the literature, sound and television master controls, audio and video duplication as well as a workshop and a kitchen. (Above) Lawrence works to duplicate audiocassettes, while in another module Lisa works on images of the crusade that will be sent by satellite phone to prayer partners around the world.

Our God is also a consuming fire!
For many people, salvation includes
turning their backs on traditional
witchcraft. At every crusade, there is
an opportunity to burn fetishes and

The *Great Gospel Crusade* in Ile-Ife, city of the royal house of Ife, seat of the king of the Yoruba people, saw a mighty harvest of souls, countless miracles, and the building of unprecedented church unity in the area.

A pall of smoke hangs over the crowd as fetishes burn in the fire. Voices are raised in jubilant praise as witchcraft and idol worship items are destroyed. Local singers and worship groups lead the huge crowd in songs that celebrate the destruction of the symbols and tools of the enemy. The entire crowd moves to the contagious rhythm of Africa, and dust rises from the dry crusade ground.

It is a rare privilege for anyone to hear so many people singing together. Sometimes, when over one million people are present, it is as if all of creation is praising its creator.

(Left) The old crusade sound system, now superseded by the new twin tower facility, will continue to be used for overflow, or *Fire Conferences*. Although highly effective in reaching large gatherings, it has simply become too small for the huge crowds that we see today.

(Right) During the week, prayer requests are gathered from across the crusade ground, and then, on the last day of the campaign, they are prayed over. Senior local pastors come onto the platform, and Reinhard Bonnke leads the entire congregation in prayer. Prayer partner requests are also brought from CfaN offices around the world and added to the prayer boxes.

Accompanied on stage by a local translator and surrounded by a sea of faces, Reinhard Bonnke speaks right to the heart of the people.

He will preach the gospel message for five nights and three days. Each night, as the crowd levels increase there is a fresh confidence and spontaneity in the praise and worship from the people, which builds to a crescendo on the final night.

'Bonnke', as the crowd calls him, preaches to his beloved Africa come rain or sun, good weather or bad, in the 'Hammatan' dust that blows in from the Sahara, or when surrounded by swarms of biting insects attracted to the powerful lights, and ... in all circumstances, 'in season and out of season'. This is his heart, and the fulfillment of his God-given vision. It is what he is called to... to Plunder Hell and Populate Heaven, and to win Africa for Jesus!

Flamboyant African dresses and tribal markings add splashes of color and style to the otherwise often poor and dusty surroundings.

Each campaign is a regional highlight and social event. The majority of those who attend will never have experienced such a huge gathering.

As the day comes to a close in West Africa, a whole new life has started for countless thousands, and often millions, of new believers who have come to know Jesus through a Reinhard Bonnke *Great Gospel Crusade.*

The huge crowd stands almost motionless as they listen to every single word of the evening's sermon, responding to the evangelist's powerful parables and teaching of the Word of God with the now familiar African exclamation of *'Eeeh!'*

The moment that Reinhard Bonnke walks off the platform for the last time, the long process of taking everything down begins. It will take at least a dozen engineers and probably a hundred or so local workers hours to complete. It is the only night that the 'Tech Team' does not eat with the rest of the team; instead, they stay at the site until the job is done.

There are thousands of individual components, speakers, cables, amplifiers, brackets, and bits and pieces, all of which need to be carefully re-packed, and stacked into the trucks ready to move on to the next *Great Gospel Crusade*, in another city, on another day.

From the time that Reinhard Bonnke and the international team leave Lagos on the Tuesday prior to the start of the crusade, they have an elite military escort/protection team all the way to the crusade site, which may be a four-hour journey away by road.

City traffic also is only negotiable with blue-light-flashing and siren-sounding escorts, which accompany the convoy (sometimes as many as fifteen vehicles) through the hustle and bustle of crowded streets.

There are numerous members of the team, both fulltime and freelance, who work together, often under difficult circumstances, to make each *Great Gospel Crusade* possible. Handling the logistics of just one event is like coordinating a military operation. With containers of literature coming in from China, technical equipment from the USA and UK, trucks that drive across some of Africa's worst roads, and team members arriving literally from all over the world, it is a true credit to the entire team each time an event takes place.

Because the *Great Gospel Crusades* are often in out-of-the-way places, we generally take our own chefs and kitchen staff, as well as a washing machine and laundry-assistant from Lagos. They bring with them CfaN's own stoves, refrigerators, crockery, cutlery, and foodstuff. Sometimes the accommodation is quite basic, and often a team of cleaners and repairmen has to go on ahead to prepare the way.

(Top) Reinhard lunches with part of the crusade team.
(Center) Adrian Bradshaw, reporter at work.
(Bottom) Kwesi, Pascal, Lawrence, and Michael, all Nigerian team members.

Morning devotions during a crusade are a highlight, and bring the entire crusade team together. On the Sunday morning, a breaking-of-bread service is held. This is often the only time during an otherwise busy week when Reinhard Bonnke has an opportunity to share his heart with the CfaN team and other visitors, who have come to experience a crusade first hand.

Photographers

This book is a compilation of images taken by a number of CfaN full-time and freelance photographers who covered the 2002/2003 crusade season. Most are from this period, but there are one or two photographs from previous events.

As far as possible, we have tried to accredit images to the respective photographer, but please forgive any incorrectly allocated. The book is a tribute to all who have contributed in some way, through its images, origination, and publication.

All images in this book were taken by Rob Birkbeck with the exception of those listed below. Most were taken on Kodak VS100, or Fuji Provia 400F using a selection of Nikon and Noblex panorama cameras. Others were captured on a Nikon D100.

Mark Theisinger: 1, 4, 6, 21b, 23b, 24c, 27b, 28, 30a, 30c, 32a, 33b, 37, 40, 46b, 49a, 50, 52a, 52b, 53a, 61a, 61b, 66a, 66b, 66c, 77, 80.
Vanessa Birkbeck: 68.
Peter van den Berg: 45, 54a, 65b.
Robert Russell: 17.
Adelmo Raymann: 87a. (Above)

(Above) Rob Birkbeck up the 'Genie' photo platform.
(Below) Mark Theisinger, on location.